Everyday MAGICK

for Children of Earth-Based Spiritual Families

Written & Illustrated by
Rayne Storm

4880 Lower Valley Road, Atglen, Pennsylvania 19310

Schiffer Books are available at special discounts for bulk purchases for sales promotions or premiums. Special editions, including personalized covers, corporate imprints, and excerpts can be created in large quantities for special needs. For more information contact the publisher:

Published by Schifffer Publishing Ltd.
4880 Lower Valley Road
Atglen, PA 19310
phone: (610) 593-1777; Fax: (610) 593-2002
E-mail: Info@schifferbooks.com

Please visit our web site catalog at
www.schifferbooks.com

We are always looking for people to write books on new and related subjects. If you have an idea for a book, please contact us at
proposals@schifferbooks.com

This book may be purchased from the publisher.
Include $5.00 for shipping.
Please try your bookstore first.
You may write for a free catalog.

In Europe, Schiffer books are distributed by:
Bushwood Books
6 Marksbury Ave.
Kew Gardens
Surrey TW9 4JF England
Phone: 44 (0) 208 392-8585
Fax: 44 (0)208 392-9876
E-mail: Info@bushwoodbooks.co.uk
Website: www.bushwoodbooks.co.uk

Design concept by Rayne Storm
Cover concept by Rayne Storm
Designed by Mark David Bowyer
Type set in Albertus Medium / Gill Sans

ISBN: 978-0-7643-4017-8
Printed in China

Kid Tested, Mother Approved...
Hearth Witch Blessed!

I so am excited that you have chosen to include my book, *Everyday Magick for Children of Earth-Based Spiritual Families*, into your family. This book is for anyone, any family, but was primarily created for families of Earth-Based spiritual beliefs – including but not limited to; Pagans, Witches, Wiccans... for Family Trads, Covens, and Solitaries too.

The following is just my little informational note, which is intended for all my readers, be you young or old... for those of you who are just curious, those of you who are new to this path, and even those who have circled 'round the grove a few times.

I feel it is necessary to do some explaining. I understand and accept, as should you, that there are different variations in traditions, pronunciations, and terms. I hope that I have kept the contents of this book *loose* enough, so that everyone can enjoy it and at the same time be *enchanted*. I hope that you are able to open your eyes (even your third eye) to the Magick that happens all around us and the Magick that we ourselves create.

While we are on the subject, let me take a quick moment to explain the word *Magick*, which you can see I spell with a "k" to differentiate between "Magic," which is slight of hand, mere parlor tricks and "Magick" which is Universal Quantum Energy / Spirituality. Not everyone chooses to differentiate the word.

I feel children of earth-based spiritualities should have the same opportunity for resources as other religions and belief systems... This is the path in life, that I walk. Understandably, my thoughts are not *omniscient wisdom,* but my journey in life has lead me here to help children embrace a growing spiritual belief, one that takes us on a journey – parallel to the path of the ancient ones.

Within the pages of this book you will find Magickal poems with corresponding activities and questions to get your child(ren) thinking, asking questions, and doing more. There is a Glossary in the back of this book to help answer any questions. Note: Content, like references to the Sabbots, are relevant to the Northern Hemisphere.

Each page was Kid tested: reviewed and read to and by children. Each page was Mother Approved by Mothers of Multiple Spiritual/Religious backgrounds. Each page has my Hearth Witch, Soul and Blessing, backing it... to be the very best, and to be grounded in fundamental principles... with deep issues translated into simple concepts for children.

I hope you and your children enjoy this collection of poems for generations to come.

HUGS
Rayne Storm

For more visit:
www.theMagickalCauldron.com

Contents

By Title / First Line

What is MAGICK?

Magick is in what we think
And what we do,
Making energy we all share and use!

We should never use Magick
To be miserable or cruel,
As we should always remember
The most basic rule:

"If what we think and what we do,
Will not harm a soul... not a one...
Then practicing Magick can be done!"

SMILE!! *(pssst.... Pass it on!)*

Smiling is one of the simplest forms of magick that anyone can practice. It not only makes you feel good inside, but it can even make others smile too. Now, just imagine, if one person tried on a smile and then a another person tried one on too, because they saw the first person wearing one... and then another person did the same.... and another.... what a world of difference that could do. ☺

QUESTION: Do you know of another form of magick, that most people practice ritually?

Answer: Praying

There is MAGICK in Prayer...

We can send one anywhere,
At anytime... or in a rhyme.

Said aloud or in our mind,
With eyes closed or open wide.

We say one when we
Need some help or time to heal,
We even say one with our meal!

We get to talk... one-on-one,
Because praying is for everyone!

SEND IT BY AIR MAIL...

Put a prayer or special note (without last names and personal details) on a small piece of paper, put it into a biodegradable latex, eco-friendly balloon and blow up the balloon. Then tie it off and add some ribbon for a tail. Now send it off, up into the sky, with one last special blessing or wish. This is especially great for children who have lost a loved one, even a pet – they can send them messages by AIR MAIL.

QUESTION: Do you know of a way to send Healing Prayers through the mail?

Answer: With a Get Well Card

7

There is MAGICK in the Clouds...

Laying there in the grass, on your back...
You see a train riding along... without a track.
Beyond that, a giant castle...
And a duck wearing a hat... that has a tassel?

Like a parade, the clouds float by...
Up next was an elephant wearing a bow-tie,
Followed by a dragon making stir-fry...
And... was that an elf, trying to sneak by?

You want to stay there all day long, watching clouds...
But your Daddy says, "That's not allowed."
That you have to come in, "There are things we must do."
In protest you whine, "Awe... Dad, do I have to?"

IMAGINATION... CREATIVITY... WHERE ARE YOU?

Being creative does not always come when you call it, like you would your puppy, nor does it stay for long periods of time, in one spot, like a sleeping cat. No! Creativity is more like fluffy clouds; they come and go. Sometimes quickly and sometimes slow. Sometimes you have lots of ideas and some days you have none. And sometimes all you can do is watch them float by... up in the sky.

QUESTION: Do you know the name for the group of 9 Greek Goddesses who inspire artists, musicians, and poets too?

Answer: The Muses

8

There is MAGICK with the Sun...

The Wheel of the year goes forever 'round,
The Sun is our guide for which we are faithfully bound.

At Yule, the Newborn Sun, does once again return.
At Imbolc, Mother Earth begins to churn.
At Ostara, springtime begins to blossom.
At Beltane, God and Goddess
Come together in a love, that is awesome!
At Litha the Sun God is at his strongest.
At Lughnassdh we begin to harvest.
At Mabon we have a feast of Thanksgiving.
At Samhain we remember... all those not living.

And, the Wheel of the Year goes forever 'round...

SUN... SUN, EVERYWHERE AND NOT A CLOUD IN SIGHT!!

Even though it would be nice to have a warm sunshine everyday, we must remember that everything in nature has to have balance. Sometimes this balance comes in the form of nice, soaking rains for our plants to drink from; other times, whether we like it or not, the balance comes in the form of cleansing and devastation... like wild fires and even hurricanes.

QUESTION: What are other names for Yule? What are other names for Litha?

Answer: Yule: Winter Solstice or Mid-Winter. Litha: Summer Solstice or Mid-Summer

There is MAGICK beneath the Full Moon...

As the Horned Owls screech with glee,
And the Bats gather in the tops of trees...

The Foxes have already began their tricksting played,
Because the Raccoons thought there was a masquerade.

The Fireflies flickered and flashed in array,
Even the Skunks couldn't be kept away.

All the while the Wolves sang a howling tune,
For the Pagans dancing beneath the Full Moon.

ONCE IN A BLUE MOON...

To say something happens "Once in a Blue Moon" means that it doesn't happen very often. It is actually the second full moon in a calendar month. Can the moon really appear blue? Not really, though sometimes the dust in the atmosphere can give the moon a bluish hue.

QUESTION: What other color can the Full Moon appear to be?

Answer: The Harvest Moon is known for having a reddish appearance

There is MAGICK in Earth...
With every seedlings birth.

There is MAGICK in Water...
Blessing each son and daughter.

There is MAGICK in Air...
With every verse chanted with flair.

There is MAGICK in Fire...
With flames that flicker with desire.

There is MAGICK in the Divine...
Marked with candles lit in shrines.

IT'S ELEMENTAL...

In a Pentagram (a five-pointed star with the point facing straight up), each point represents a different element. Starting at the top most point, you have Spirit (the Divine), then going clockwise (to the right) you have Water, Fire, Earth, Air, and back to Spirit at the top. Take a moment to recognize all the elements around you, how many can you find?

QUESTION: Can you name the 5 Chinese Elements? (Hint: 3 of the elements are the same as above.)

Answer: Wood, Metal, Water, Earth, and Fire

There is MAGICK in a Tiny Seed...
That grows up to be a BIG tree,
Who will share this world with you and me.

There is MAGICK in a Buzzy Bee...
To make honey for you and me,
From all the beautiful flowers that we see.

There is MAGICK in all Animals...
No matter how BIG or how small,
Each with a little something to teach us all.

MAGICK is in the Food We Eat...
Like carrots, broccoli, and beets...
Plus, apples, corn, potatoes, and wheat.

IT'S THE LITTLE THINGS...
Have you ever stopped to smell the wild flowers, or to take a closer look at a pinecone? Have you ever waited for a snail to cross your path? Have you ever just stood still... to see what wonders are nearby... to wait for creatures to flutter by?

CHALLENGE: To notice the many different kinds of Insects, Plants, Trees, and Animals. What are some of your favorite animals or wonders in Nature?

There is MAGICK in seeing a Mermaid...

Waving Hi!
With her tail as she playfully swims by.

There is MAGICK in glimpsing a Gnome...

In an overgrown garden of old,
Privileged to you, a rare site to behold.

There is MAGICK in finding a Faery...

Talking rhyme,
Beneath the sprigs of Mommy's thyme.

There is MAGICK in flying with a Dragon...

Majestically up he soars,
Before swooping down to the Earthen floor.

TO BELIEVE OR NOT TO BELIEVE...

If you Believe in something, then IT DOES Exist! If you Don't Believe in it, than it DOES NOT Exist! So that monster, under your bed... DOES NOT exist... It might just be your Guardian Dragon, if you BELIEVE it to be so. And those strange noises, are just the noises a dragon makes when he is trying to get cozy under your bed. Next time, when he thumps under your bed... why not invite him up, to sleep with you!

CHALLENGE: To think about what you believe in. When you close your eyes and open your mind, what do you see... What do you believe?

There is MAGICK in a Winter Snow...

Each Flake, so fluffy and white
Dancing and Playing, while in flight
Swirling and Twirling all about
And there is no doubt
How you'd spend the day...
All you want to do is go out and play
Making snowmen and snowballs
Until your Mother calls.

WE ARE ALL ONE OF A KIND AND UNIQUE...

Snowflakes all have 6 sides, but not one – not even one of them – are alike. Each snowflake looks similar, but they are not exactly the same! Have everyone in your family make a snowflake, without templates and patterns. Decorate them, add their name to their snowflake, and hang them all from a paper chain. Sit back and enjoy your beautiful snowflake garland.

QUESTION: What do you notice about your Family Snowflake Garland?

Answers may vary: They are all unique, wonderful, special and one of a kind!

There is MAGICK in a Spring Rain...

The rain drips... drips down in a muddle,
Dancing playfully atop the mud puddles...
Excited about the prospects of spring,
And the wonderful flowers it shall bring...
You watch from your dry confines...
Wanting to be apart of the redesign...
To play in a fresh Spring rain blissfully,
As the earth turns green with dignity...
Becoming greener with colorful bouquets
Washing away the dreary winter grays.

TWO SEASONS or FOUR SEASONS...

Most everyone, when asked, will tell you that there are four seasons: Winter, Spring, Summer, and Autumn (Fall). But in ancient times, the Celts really only had two seasons: Winter and Summer. Winter was the cold season, also known as the season of darkness. Summer was the hot season, also known as the season light.

QUESTION: The Celtic people changed seasons at the point of Equinox. What are the two Equinoxes?

Answer: Vernal (Spring) Equinox and Autumnal (Fall) Equinox

There is MAGICK in the Summer Sun...

It seems like an eternity
since we last felt the sun,
To run barefoot across
an open field just for fun.
Winter's dry air and
whipping winds have taken their toll
And we crave the sun's warmth,
right down into our souls.
Our winter complaints
seem to melt away
Feeling better, feeling stronger...
a little more each day.
We bask like cats and play like pups,
With renewed energy and playfulness, we soak it up!

NATURAL SUNSCREEN TO ULTRAVIOLET (UV) RADIATION...

UV radiation is found in sunlight. The Earth's protective Ozone blocks the majority of this UV radiation, but our bodies protect us too. As the UV radiation touches our skin (in moderation), it increases the amount of brown pigment or melanin in the skin, creating a sun tan. The melanin absorbs the UV radiation – blocking it from our body – but too much UV radiation causes a sun burn, damaging skin tissue.

QUESTION: What else happens if you have too much and too little exposure?

Answers: Too Much: Destroys Vitamin A in the body. Too Little: You can suffer from a lack of Vitamin D

16

There is MAGICK in Autumn Leaves...

The cold north winds, give the shivers to the trees
Changing the colors of their leaves.

Down they fall, trickling down with grace
At a slow but steady pace.

Swirling and Twirling about, the leaves do play...
Until at last... they are so tired... that down they lay.

Then, children in their knitted sweaters and wool hats
Make piles, from their leaf-covered lawn mats.

IT'S DECIDUOUS....

There are two different kids of trees, Deciduous and Evergreen Trees. Deciduous trees drop their leaves during the year, usually in the fall and Evergreen trees stay forever green, throughout the year. Take time in the fall to go around finding different kinds of leaves. Maybe even create some beautiful leaf rubbings – to preserve them.

QUESTION: **What do the Deciduous and Evergreen trees have in common?**

Answers may vary: They both drop seeds, like pinecones and "helicopters"!

17

There is MAGICK in Rainbows...

As they appear magickally in the sky,
There is a brief moment... whereby
The dreary rain and the sunny sky, do so bring...
A little bit of wonderful, to every little thing.

There is MAGICK in Rainbows...
Chasing after Leprechauns, for pots of gold
Dreaming about fortunes, in stories foretold.

COLORS OF THE RAINBOW...

If you look closely, you will see that there are actually seven colors that make up a rainbow; Red, Orange, Yellow, Green, Blue, Indigo, and Violet. The colors and shape of the rainbow form as the sunlight passes through the raindrops, refracting it, changing the direction of it. There is almost always a rainbow, even a faint one, when it is raining and the sun is shinning, at the same time.

QUESTION: How can you create a Rainbow, indoors, without any rain?

Answers may vary: By passing sunlight through a prism

There is MAGICK in Surprises...

It lies in the slight chance of not knowing...
When the suspense of the unknown... begins growing.
It's then that the heart races with anticipation,
And the hairs on your arm react to the sensation...
As you surmise...   your SURPRISE!

There is MAGICK in Surprises...
It's when we have absolutely no idea, whatsoever...
Of the wonders that await us in our life endeavours.

SURPRISE... SURPRISE, WHAT A SWEET SURPRISE!

Did you know that Honey has many healthy benefits? When taken it helps with pollen allergies, it is an excellent source of carbohydrates (which gives you energy). It helps you fight off diseases and infections, and is used to help to treat and soothe soar throats. When applied directly, honey can help to treat minor cuts and burns. (However, it is advised that children under two years of age, should NOT be given honey!)

QUESTION: Can you name one of the many cousins to the Honey Bee?

Answers may vary: Bumble bees, Carpenter bees, Orchid bees

There is MAGICK in Your Soul...

Inside all of us is something very unique,
Beyond the confines of our physique...
Our souls are a lock box... a treasure trove
And if we seek out our inner cove
We will find answers to questions...
Tips, advice, and some suggestions...

We have within us... one soul
With a divine scroll
Listing all the lives we've lived, we've toured...
And all the lessons we've endured.

That's why our greatest quest... is always and forever...
To Love and to Live! You should make it your endeavour!

GOING ON A SPIRITUAL QUEST!!!

I'm going on a Special Quest! It's going to be a Spiritual Quest!! So, who's going with me?
How about you? Will you go with me?
Going to give Love with an open heart! Going to share my gifts, and my blessings too!!
So, who will join me? Who wants to live their life; is it you?

QUESTION: People have been going on quests, since the beginning of time, for many different reasons... can you name any?

Answers may vary: searching for the fountain of youth

There is MAGICK in a Moonrise...

Once the sun has set, and darkness lingers in its place...
The glittering stars begin to brighten up the empty space.
The moon shines big and bright, hanging in the sky,
Watching over us with tribute... from up above so high.

There is MAGICK in a Sunrise...

It greets us everyday, without fail,
To rise above every mountain and boat sail...
To give us light and warmth with its rays
Even if it is a bit tame... on rainy days.

PUTTING YOUR DAY TO BED....

Many ancients believed that you had to put your day away, before you could go to bed, before nightfall. They saw the time between the daylight and the coming darkness, as being the beginning of the next day. All that needed to be done, was to be done before dusk, therefore leaving you ready to go to bed, without worries, and getting a good night sleep... which in turn would leave you refreshed and energized to begin again in the daylight!

QUESTION: Which came first: the Darkness of Chaos – or – the Warmth of Love and of Light?

Answers may vary: Light was born out of the Darkness

There is MAGICK in the Newborn Sun...

On a cold, dark, and blustery night... amid winter's jaws
Came a jolly old man whom they called, Shaman Claus.
He was dressed in red wool from his head to his toes
And his beard was as white as the falling snow.
He had a special delivery that had to be done...
He was to help with the arrival of the newborn sun...
Goddess arrived in a heavenly gown... as black as night...
Yet it sparkled and shimmered with starlight.
It was then, that the newborn
Sun God was born... of love and of light,
Shattering the darkness
with his golden rays... so, refreshingly bright!
Goddess gave us all a gift...
that of a precious newborn
Whose warm embrace hugs us
one and all on this... the Solstice morn!

HELLO SUN!!

Yule or WInter Solstice, signifies the return or birth of the newborn Sun/the Sun God. Since the beginning of time, cultures from around the world have worshiped and honored him. He is known by many names, such as: Ra (Egyptian), Helios (Greek), and Sol (Roman).

RITUAL CHALLENGE:
To create a morning yoga-like stretch routine to greet the Sun God and to awaken yourself. (To practise even on rainy days – because God is always there with us, even if we don't see him.)

There is MAGICK in Candlelight...

Even though light is slowly returning to us,
There is still a cold overcast that makes us all fuss.
There was a time, long ago, when candles burned bright,
Giving hope that everything would be alright.
Because Imbolc is the promise of nearing Spring
When nature begins to stir and the birds joyously sing.
It is a time for a candlelight celebration,
With a ritual for coming out of hibernation.
It is a time for making predictions about spring
And a time for spring cleaning – cleaning out everything!
Focus on Goddess's love in the candlelight;
Feel her warmth, even in the dark of night...
Fire feeds our soul and warms our heart,
Pushing the darkness out, so it does depart!

OH, WHERE... OH, WHERE CAN SPRING BE?!

Imbolc is six weeks after Yule, and though it is the first of three spring celebrations, many people are still digging out from under snow and feeling the overwhelming linger of their anticipation of green grass again. In many traditions, Brighid (Celtic) is viewed as the Mother aspect, and is associated with the Hearth and Home at Imbolc – she kept the Home fires burning. For without light... there was only darkness.

RITUAL CHALLENGE: To create and plan an Imbolc party to help shake off the winter gray. Maybe the theme could be tropical... and you could make up games like Pin the Shadow on the Groundhog.

There is MAGICK in a Little Sprout...

That was once, without a doubt,
First a helicopter, holding onto a little seed.
That dropped in early autumn, from a Maple tree.
Protected by the falling leaves,
Laying quiet in the eaves.
Sleeping soundly beneath a winter's snowing,
Awaiting Ostara's warm spring winds a blowing.
Awakening and rising from the ground,
With his tiny leaves wrapped 'round.
Then, carefully stretching out wide,
Soaking up the sun's warmth with pride.
This little sprout, that was once a seed,
Can't wait to know what he is destined to be.

DO BUNNIES LAY EGGS?

The only known bunny to lay eggs is Ostara's bunny (also known as the Easter Bunny). Legend says that Ostara found an injured bird laying in the cold, cold, snow – because she knew he would never fly again, she transformed him into a bunny. He was so grateful for a second chance at life that every year he would lay 13 colorful eggs, to honor Ostara.

RITUAL CHALLENGE: To create a new tradition in honor of Ostara and her compassion for animals. Be sure to include the coloring of hardboiled or blown eggs to honor Ostara, and the new seedlings and sprouts of spring, as well.

There is MAGICK in Spinning...

Round and round the dancers dance with soul,
With ebb and with flow around the maypole
Weaving in... out... and around
Spinning, twirling... falling to the ground.
Can you hear the drum-drumming
Ever so slightly it quickens in forthcoming
And the dancers match its beat ... with their feet...
As the music rises in the air,
There the energy creates a love affair...
They welcome in the summer sun
With good food, family, friends, and fun!!!

IN WITH THE OLD!

Sometimes we loose sight of the ways of old, while in our modern little boxes. Traditions that if not practiced, or remembered, will surely be forgotten... to become nothing. A Traditional Beltane celebration would have included a Maypole, with its ribbons, a Maypole dance, and many decorations using Spring flowers.

RITUAL CHALLENGE: To learn more about the Maypole and its dance. Then using some ribbon or crepe paper, create a family Maypole around a tree or a pole. Invite others over to partake in this joyous Springtime tradition.

There is MAGICK in Bonfires...

Whether you are camping out... with a campfire,
Eating marshmallows that you set slightly afire...
Or in your backyard with everyone gathered 'round
Telling spooky stories – feeling your heart as it begins to pound...
It is now that you can say,
That summer is here to stay...
At least for a little while...
Or while swimwear is still in style.
The flames of the fire
(Do flicker and flash)
As we watch and admire
(It crackles and pops)
Speaking a language all of its own...
(Quietly sitting and staring)
We become drawn into the unknown...

THE SUMMER SOLSTICE!

The Summer Solstice is also referred to as Mid-summer... though for many, in the northern areas, it is just the beginning of better weather. Solstice actually means 'sun - stands still,' in which is does, for that day. It is also the point that daylight begins to gradually become less and less, that is until the Winter Solstice – when it begins its return again.

RITUAL CHALLENGE: To create a Summer Solstice Adventure, one that will become a yearly tradition of summer fun, with games, treats and treasure hunts, and a good ol' bonfire.... with marshmallows of course!

There is MAGICK in the Fields...

Producing food in yields
When fruits and vegetables are at their peak,
You go out to the fields each week.
And pick as much as you possibly can
And though it may seem hectic, there is a plan
To fill barrels, bushels, baskets, and bags too...
Plus the little pints filled with berries of red and blue.
So many tasty things to eat... and all are a healthy treat!

HARVEST TIME BEGINS WITH LUGHNASADH!

Lughnasadh is the first of the three harvest celebrations. In some areas, fruits and vegetables can be picked earlier, with multiple plantings of that crop... but in some areas, they are just beginning to see the real "Wheat and Beans" of their hard work. Lughnasadh is traditionally centered around the harvesting of Wheat, to which they made bread. It was considered a necessity in meals – all year long.

RITUAL CHALLENGE: To learn more about bread making, and to even make a loaf yourself (even if it's a small loaf). Then during your Lughnasadh celebration with friends and family, enjoy a celebration with the bread you created, just as the ancients would have.

There is MAGICK in a Harvest Feast...

Spending hours in the garden till we are worn
Harvesting tomatoes, potatoes, and corn,
Making pickled cucumbers and beets
Oh, such mouth watering treats.

The changing of the leaves does portend,
As our gardens near their end.
But before the snow settles in,
We gather with our kith and kin...
Giving thanks for all we hold dear...
Being polite, respectful, and sincere,
For good food, friends, and so much more,
Which is the way... since the time of lore.

GIVING THANKS!

Mabon is the second of the Harvest celebrations, in which we show thanks and give thanks for our food, our crops, our family, and our friends. Traditionally, this Sabbot is celebrated, as a Thanksgiving Feast, in September. Other countries/cultures celebrate it in October (Canada) and November (United States).

RITUAL CHALLENGE: To create a new dinner or meal prayer. Maybe have one that's just for Sabbot celebrations, and a simple one, that's multi-religious, and/or for everyday meals.

28

There is MAGICK on All Hallows Eve...

Once a year... for just one night
All the little children get the green light
To dress up and pretend to be... Anything!
Like a bellowing Banshee or a courageous King...
A terrible Troll.. or a sassy little Sprite...
So many choices... so many creatures of the night...

Pumpkins, scarecrows, and ghosts... Oh, MY!
Goblins and other creatures lurking nearby...
Candy is what these little creatures seek...
Seeking out... with a door-to-door technique...
But beware the words... *"Trick or Treat!"*
'Cause they won't retreat... without their treat!

SCARECROWS... PUMPKINS... AND SPIRITS!! OH, MY!

Did you know that Samhain is considered to be the day when the gateway between this world and the otherworld is the thinnest, meaning we can communicate with the spirit world better. Children use to dress up as ghosts and other – otherworld creatures – in order to make the otherworld spirits feel more welcomed in this world.

RITUAL CHALLENGE: To create and plan a ritual costume dance party and invite all your friends and family from this world and the otherworld, to join you in a Spook-tacular party.

There is MAGICK in a Smile...
When we excitedly rejoice,
Or when we use a pleasant tone of voice.

There is MAGICK in a Smile...
Be it with lips sweetly sealed,
Or with a great big grin that is revealed.

There is MAGICK in a Smile...
That brightens up a day,
Allowing good things to come our way...
And when everyday things go our way,
We spread happiness in a contagious way.

THE ACT OF SMILING!

The act of smiling does not mean you should fake or pretend to smile. To "act" means "to do"... so we need to do a lot more smiling! There are different kinds of smiles; we smile when we love someone or something, when we are happy to see someone, when things are going good, and we even smile when we sleep. However, when we smile because we feel uncomfortable.... That's actually a grimace, not a smile.

CHALLENGE: To make at least one person, anyone, someone... at least once everyday... SMILE! How do they feel? And what about you? How do you feel?

There is MAGICK in Comfort Food...
It's a subtle friend when our nose runs a bit,
And our sneezes won't quit...
When we cough... we begin to **whoop**...
And mama makes us some chicken noodle soup.

There is MAGICK in Comfort Food...
It's a good friend when your ankle you bruise...
In a game you just couldn't loose...
But then the rain turned the field into a stream,
And daddy made the call, to go get some ice cream!

YUM!!!
We all have our favorite foods! Some good for us... some not so much. Sometimes we eat when we are sad, mad, or glad. But remember, too much of a good thing isn't a good thing; everything should be eaten in moderation, in smaller portions... and always eat slowly so you can at least enjoy what you are eating... because before you know it, it will be all gone – and you'll want more.

CHALLENGE: To collect family favorite recipes to create an heirloom family cookbook. Design unique borders for your recipes. And be sure to put their names with the entries!

There is MAGICK in the Desert...

With its FIRE hot hills of granulated sand...
You are likely to get more than just a tan,
With its hot temperatures and dry air...
You wouldn't want to run around bare.
With a scorching sun that sizzles and sears...
Don't be surprised if a mirage appears.

There is MAGICK in an Oasis...

With its lush vegetation and palm trees...
And its cool WATERS and warm breeze
Sharing space with a giant sand box...
Supplying water to each camel and desert fox
A hidden little paradise... it is its own isle...
A wondrous adventure, that makes it worthwhile.

IS IT MIRAGE OR A MIRACLE?

A mirage is an optical illusion... what your brain thinks your eyes see... it really is just an illusion, it's not there... and it's not likely to materialize, to come about. Where as miracles are usually considered to be of a divine act. Confusion comes from the thought, or lack of faith, one has in miracles. If you can't, won't, or don't believe in miracles... then the outcome you seek... is nothing more then a mirage.

QUESTION: There are three requirements to creating a miracle: Believe in yourself, focus on your intent (the miracle you wish to create) ...and... ?

Answers may vary: Have Faith in the Divine

There is MAGICK in the Mountains...

You'll find rock ledges and a thick evergreen covering...
And clouds that gather around... just hovering
Seen reaching down to earth... it is no illusion
Creating a natural infusion...
Breathe in deeply the AIR of content...
It is a crisp, clean mountain scent!

There is MAGICK in a Cave...

A perplexing maze... an in-depth labyrinth system...
With a secretively enchanting... Elven kingdom...
Flickering shadows of light guide the way
Through tunnels that could lead you astray
Deeper into darkness... into the EARTH you diverge...
Potentially lost...   you hope that an elf will emerge!

GETTING LOST... TO BE FOUND

A Labyrinth uses a system of paths for meditation. It gives each person an individual experience. Each and every walk will be a different experience. As you walk... you are setting aside time for yourself to ground and center... to reflect upon daily activities and to think through troubling thoughts and issues that have you feeling lost... walking the labyrinth until the answers that are sought... become found.

QUESTION: A labyrinth is a geometrically shaped sacred space where magick takes place. Can you name an ancient space or place that is similar ?

Answers may vary: Stonehedge

There is MAGICK when you Believe...

Knowing that anything is possible...
When the thought of the impossible...
Is pushed aside without a doubt
So good things can come about.
When you put all your trust...
(*...and you must...*)
...In what lies within you,
You can make dreams come true.
It's a power kept safe in your soul
That helps play an important role,
Simply have a goal to achieve
And all you have to do... to receive...
Is to focus on Love and on Light,
And truly Believe with all your might!

THE MAGICK OF A BOX...

Boxes can hold so many things! Like trinkets, tidbits and many a thingamajig. We keep them around because they keep safe ...some of our most important things... things you just can't throw away. The box becomes an object that reminds us of so many things... memories that are still alive and well... deep inside ourselves!

CHALLENGE: Write down some special requests for change, and place them into a Magickal Box for safe keeping – to keep the belief that the requests for change will be created.

There is MAGICK when you Give...

No matter what you desire,
What you would like to acquire...
There is a simple rule
(*...just like you'd have at school...*)
To make your desire come about
First off... you must be devout...
Giving love with an open heart,
Is the only place for you to start.

Then before you know it
Love and light, you will emit...
Leaving you feeling awesome inside...
Ready to gladly give again with pride.
For giving love openly, like you do...
Trust that, love will find its way to you.

PAY IT FORWARD...

Pay it Forward is an expression used to represent the act of having someone re-pay you for your help... but instead of paying in monies, they put their appreciation back into helping someone else... and then having the person they helped, help someone else... and on and on... always paying back by passing it forward.

CHALLENGE: Create a Pay It Forward Day. A day that you and your friends and family, help others – and in return ask ONLY that they pass on the same kindness they were shown.

There is MAGICK in Karma...

What is Karma, you so innocently question?
Well, you see, on your soul... there is an impression...
And what you say, think, and how you interact
With people, pets, places, and plants... are tracked
From one lifetime into the next... it's carried with you...
Be it good or bad, it always knows where to find you.
It's there to guide us like an adviser...
Encouraging us to become more loving and wiser.
So, let your heart be open to Love and Light
And your mind to common sense, so that it can find sight.
Let your soul be your intuition, your all-knowing...
And nothing will be sacrificed, nothing forgoing...
Nothing bestowed upon you... you didn't deserve...
Karma is your personal energy... that's here to observe...
It twirls, whirls, and swirls... all around...
Before every bit of it... is written down!

RIGHT UNDER YOUR NOSE...

Did you ever notice that little indent, right under your nose? They say, that each time we come back... we have with us all the memories of past lives, and the answers to what comes after life... but such things shouldn't be told or there would be nothing left to be amazed and surprised with... so when we are sent back... to this world... a simple kiss on the end of a Divine finger... seals our lips... sealing in the secrets.

CHALLENGE:
Cultures have been creating stories to explain and teach about things in life. Create your own explanation story.

There is MAGICK in Dharma...

We all have a purpose, a Dharma...
In addition to our Karma...
We are all blessed with this gift, before our birth...
Even before our souls reach the earth.
Whether we know our plot... whether we accept it or not...
That's why you are here... it was whispered into your ear.

It is a gift to share with the few... or the umpteen...
Sometimes it is years before we know the unseen,
Then again, sometimes we find our place...
Or rather, we think we've found our space
But we still have much to learn and do...
This sacred gift was given to you...
To appreciate, develop and to ultimately share...
Leaving you blissful... feeling like you are walking on air!

WHAT IS, WILL BE...

To many Buddhists, Dharma refers to the natural law of things. In Hinduism, it is used to explain one's personal obligations or calling. In the new age, it is most often used to explain the life path of one's soul. Your Karma is attached to your Dharma, they can never be separated... but both are influenced and changed by the everyday choices you make in this life time... each and every life you live.

RIDDLE: **Why should you live THIS moment, in this lifetime, and not dwell in past lives or future ones?**

Answer: Because it's a Present!

There is MAGICK in Peace...

Sometimes in life, there are things we can't control...
They can be as small as a knoll ... or as big as a troll....
It irritates and agitates our soul... creating a giant hole...
BUT... when we learn to accept what we can't change...
Our lives will become more peaceful, in the long range.
Seeds that contain wishes... wishing things were different,
Are scattered about the air... they are indifferent.
We will never be able to understand,
And we will never be able to... not even by demand...
Make changes about what others choose to do...
Nor can we make... or force the world to be anew...
BUT... we can take control of ourselves,
We have the power to create peace within ourselves...
It begins with acceptance... allowing happiness and peace...
To do, what it does best... make the uneasiness cease!

PEACE TALKS...

Talking Sticks or Peace Pipes are/were used in Native North American Tribes at tribal meetings. It was an object, that was designated, to allow the one in possession of it to speak freely without interruption... which also allowed others to listen. It encouraged discussion and resolutions... to make peace, not to start a war.

CHALLENGE: The idea of having an object, that allows for peaceful talking, is being used in many of today's group situations and families. Create your own family talking stick.

There is MAGICK in Dreams...

Dare to dream .... Let your inner self take flight...
Soar to new heights.... taking in each remarkable sight
Hang tight to your dragon... and soar up... and down under...
Traveling to the most fantastical places... to lands of wonder...
Walk in, around and about... the most unusual spaces...
You'll meet some interesting characters... in intriguing places...

Call to Cernunnos and he'll race you through the forest green...
Then race you back... so you can be present for the Faery Queen

Celebrate with a dance... beneath the full moon with Goddess herself...
Joining hands with nine woodland nymphs... and a merry little elf

There is many an adventure awaiting for you in your imagination...
And all you need to do is... close your eyes and begin your creation.

HOW WELL DO YOU KNOW YOURSELF?

There is much you can learn if you watch and listen to the animals around you... They teach us to be aware of people who are sly like the fox... and that there is always, at least, one black sheep in a crowd (and it might even be you)... Even knowing which animals scare you the most, can teach us something too... if you are afraid of grasshoppers... then you might be afraid of "leaping" forward in life, afraid to take risks.

CHALLENGE: Learn more about Animal Totems. Create a list of your favorite animals and your least favorite animals... what do the animals say about you... is it accurate? Be truthful to yourself.

There is MAGICK in Life...

Do you walk a bent path or run along the crooked lane?
Do you ride along the straight road and across the plain?
Do you feel like you should be climbing a mountain... for days,
Or do you enjoy getting lost in a maze?

Life is a journey of learning,
Filled with experiences, and of yearning...
With opportunities that will be bestowed,
Every time you come to a fork in the road.

Sometimes we feel we should, turn around and go back...
But always remember to continue on... and never unpack.
Life, like all living things, should always be treasured...
Because in the end, that is how we are measured.

THE THINGS I WANT TO DO LIST!

We all have goals and dreams, aspirations and ambitions, of things we would like to do, see, play, or find. Whether we write it down or not, we all keep a challenging list. Maybe you want to fly in the air, swim in the ocean, walk on the moon, or travel to the center of the Earth... Then again, maybe you have a different set of goals... like making a difference, helping out other countries or people in need.

CHALLENGE: Make a list of things you want to do in your lifetime... make it your quest, to cross off everything on your list.

There is MAGICK in Letting Go...

What do you wish? ...And don't hold out.
What do you want, without a doubt?
Make the pledge to work real hard...
Always smile, without the slightest hint of disregard.
Believe in your goal... have patience, it will unfold...
Set your mind on what the future will hold...

And now, for the hardest part... you MUST let it go!
Like the seed, that in the wind does blow...
You must LET IT GO!
Let the seeds of magick GROW!
Allowing the Spiritual Energy to do the rest,
Because that is what IT does best!

PLANTING MAGICK...

DO THE WORK: Get yourself a little seed, any seed will do. FOCUS: Make a wish on your little seed and plant it in a special home. HELP IT GROW with Tender Loving Care and BELIEVE that it will grow. LET IT GO: Once your little plant is ready, plant it outside. WAIT! Be Patient! You will soon know what grows!

CHALLENGE: What will you Grow? Make a wish, do the work then, let it go to see what grows!

There is MAGICK in Making Music...

The rain gets in sync... with *tink   tink   tink   tink*
The North wind blew... *whooooo   whooooo*
The little bird sings from his tree... *chickerdee - dee - dee*
The thunder rumbles like a bass drum... *brrrrruuuuummm*
The woodpecker adds his rap... *ta-tat tap   ta-tat tap*
And the lighting has a knack...
for sounding off with a *KKKRAAAACK!!*

The music calls to you, with an
subconscious little hum... *hhhuuummm*
And before you know it,
You're drumming... *pah-rum pum-pum pum*

Creating music all day long...
Feeling the magick with each and every song!

STRIKE UP A BEAT...

Drums are one of the oldest instruments in recorded history. They come in many different shapes and sizes, they can be made from different materials to produce different sounds too. Drums are percussive instruments. There are snare drums, hand drums, congas, bass drums, steel drums, and timpani too, just to name a few.

QUESTION: What are some other percussive instruments that aren't drums?

Answers may vary: maracas, tambourine, chimes, xylophone, triangle, cymbals

There is MAGICK in Creating Art...
Creations that come straight from your own heart!

We all have the creativity inside of us to start...
To start creating one-of-a-kind pieces of priceless art.

Crayons are great, when you want to scribble...
And when you can't paint, cause you will dribble.
Painting with your fingers and toes can be lots of fun...
But it's even better... when you are outside, in the sun!

Art should not be judged by its style or subject,
It should be displayed with pride and respect...
Caring not about what others may question...
But, by celebrating life through personal expression!!

WHICH WITCH IS WHICH?

Throughout history, Witches (and their kind) have been created in art to be ugly old women with warts. Why? Because art is created from the eye of the artist who paints or draws what they see, feel, hear and know... as do we all. With respect to the artists, it is not our place to judge their work... It is what they see and believe... however, we can begin the process of changing how artists of today view things, so that the art of tomorrow will be more respectful to all spiritual beliefs.

CHALLENGE: What is your view of things? To draw or paint what you see, feel, hear, and know about your own spiritual beliefs!

There is MAGICK
with Mommy...
When we work together in the garden... on days that are balmy.

There is MAGICK
with Daddy...
When he predicts the future... with leaves from his tea caddy.

There is MAGICK
with Sisters and Brothers...
Sometimes we are the only child and sometimes there are others.

There is MAGICK with
Grampa and Granny...
They always have something special to give... it really is uncanny!

SPECIAL ONE-ON-ONE TIME...

Everyone needs a little one-on-one time. It might be with mommy or maybe with daddy... it might even be with Grampa and Granny. It is special... very personal time... a bonding time with the family you love. But sometimes... and we all need it... we need a one-on-one time with ourselves, more of a ME time, where you take time to be by yourself.

QUESTION: **What is the name for the practice of Divination that uses tea leaves to predict the future?**

Answer: Tassology

There is MAGICK in Giggles...

Do you giggle...
Do you joyfully wriggle...
When tackled...
And delightfully tickled?

Do you squeal...
Do you feel the rush of absolute zeal...
While cheerfully twirling...
Whirling and swirling?

Do you laugh out loud...
Do you cry real tears... even in a crowd...
When something is so much more then just humorous...
It's down right, foot-stompin'... hilarious?

IT'S MORE THEN JUST A GIGGLE...

It starts with a smile... and then a quiet little chuckle. Then you try to hide that cute little giggle... that before too long breaks into laughter. That laughter spreads like a contagious sneeze... until at last you are laughing so hard, you can barely breath.... They say, laughter is the best medicine, and truthfully, it does cure many things... like a case of the Rainy Day Blues.

RIDDLE: How does Laughter cure someone who suffers from a frightful frown?

Answer: by turning it upside down!

There is MAGICK in Blowing Bubbles...

See how magickally they appear
With just a bit of blowing air

GREAT BIG ONES...
Little *tiny* ones...
Some that float up towards the sun... non-stop
And others float down... to the ground... and POP!

Bubbles provide lots of fun to go around,
Causing giggles galore with bouncing up and down

Make a game of it... create a silly plan
To chase them down... if you think you can!

YOU CAN NEVER HAVE ENOUGH BUBBLES!

Bubbles are one of the simplest, easiest, and cheapest ways to have a little fun. Little tiny babies blow bubbles with their spit, and children love to bathe when they are in a tub full of bubbles... Bubbles are used to help clean clothes in the washing machine, and they play around in a sink full of dirty dishes. You can even blow bubbles in your milk, with a straw... of course that is... if your mother says that it's okay!

QUESTION: **Using different objects as bubble wands, see how many different shapes of bubbles you can make.**

Answer: Just 1 shape, a circle

There is MAGICK in a Little Rain Cloud...

Little cloud so blue, is it true...
That all we need to do is ...*sigh*...
And have ourselves a little cry?

When life gets cluttered
And leaves us a bit fluttered
It can leave us feeling sad or mad...
Especially when there is fun to be had.
And that little rain cloud, he's sad too
He's been collecting emotions... who knew?
When we throw out our stress
It floats away... up to the sky, I guess...
Till the little cloud is gray and full of pain...
BURSTING!! Showering us with rain.

RAIN, RAIN, GO AWAY... COME AGAIN ANOTHER DAY!

Clouds actually do pick up little dust and dirt particles that are floating around in the air. They also collect moisture that's in the air... and when they have had enough... and are tired of holding on to all that dirt, dust, and water... they get dark and grumpy... and rain it all back down to Earth. But as the weather turns cold, it comes down in the form of freezing rain or even snow.

QUESTION: Can you name the two different types of STORM CLOUDS?

Answer: Nimbus (rain clouds) and Cumulus (thunderstorm clouds)

There is MAGICK in Being You...

Just be yourself, that's what it's all about!

How boring... so ho-hum,
The world would become...
It would be a tragic shame
If we were all one and the same
You should figure out... seriously think about...
Would we all be leaders... or followers?
Would we all shy away from talk...
Or would we all just continuously squawk?

Luckily, we're not equally displayed
But we are uniquely and Divinely, handmade...
So, embrace who you are... and reach for the stars
The magick is... in and of itself....
Inside of you... to Just be Yourself!!

LET'S PLAY CHARADES!!!

Charades is a game of acting out people and animals. The catch is you can't talk... not even a bark, a meow or a rib-bit.... You can't even use props or other people or objects to help you act out your secret. Your secret is what is written on a piece of paper in a hat or bucket, then you pick out one of those secrets from the hat or bucket to know what you need to act out.

CHALLENGE: Everyone should pick a secret name of a family member/pet etc., and act out that secret, while everyone else tries to guess who the secret is! See how unique we all are?

There is MAGICK in a Pocket Full...

A pocket full of Basil,
Will keep you from being nasal.

A pocket full of Thyme,
Will keep you from talking rhyme.

A pocket full of Myrrh,
Will keep away pests with fur.

A pocket full of Bay,
And friends will come to play.

A pocket full of Rose,
To help with smelly toes.

POCKET FULL OF POSIES...

Did you know that long, long ago people carried flowers, both dried and fresh, in their pockets. It was a form of perfume and body freshener in one! And they would chew on mint leaves to freshen their breath. Fragrant fresh cut flowers were used to brighten up a room and as an air freshener too. Matter of fact, we still cut fresh fragrant flowers, to fill our homes with their wonderful aromas.

CHALLENGE: With help, make a list of flowers, herbs, and trees and what they are useful for. (Like mint leaves freshen our breath)

There is MAGICK in the Everyday...

On Sunday wearing Gold,
Could get your fortune told.
On Monday wearing Silver or Gray,
Will keep you from eating a bail of hay.
On Tuesday wearing Red,
Will have you eating bread.
On Wednesday wearing Yellow,
Will have you feeling a bit mellow.
On Thursday wearing Blue,
Could get you something new.
On Friday wearing Pink,
Will make your armpits stink.
On Saturday wearing Black,
Will make you want to quack.

IT'S SUPERSTITIOUS LUCK! *(Knock on wood!)*

A superstition is something that is believed in, even if there is no rational thought, reasoning, or a proven fact to back it up... But the belief that "IT" (the superstition in question) does exist makes it real enough. So if you believe that wearing Blue on Thursday could get you something new, then by all means wear blue; it might be the luckiest thing you do... that is, if you believe in superstitions.

QUESTION: Do you know what the difference between Hay and Straw is?

Answer: Hay is dried grass and is eaten. Straw is dried stalks of cereal used as bedding.

There is MAGICK in the color White...
When we associate Deities with a sacred light.

There is MAGICK in the color Green...
When we listen to Mother Earth, with ears so keen.

There is MAGICK in the color Blue...
When there is a world of learning that is always new.

There is MAGICK in the color Yellow...
When used to brighten a day that is mellow.

There is MAGICK in the color Red...
When we believe that all our fears will be shed.

THE PENTAGRAM PATH

Our souls rest with the DIVINE, before they make their way to EARTH, as a soul to be a born. Created in WATER, in a womb and brought into this world, filling our lungs with AIR, to live out our life. And when we finally leave this world, our souls are filled to capacity with love from the Divine, warming our souls with FIRE, filling it like a hot air balloon so that our soul can float up, Up, UP... back to the DIVINE once again.

QUESTION: Can you name (one or any) the God/Goddess who looks after departed souls, for those who are between lifetimes?

Answers may vary: Hel (Norse), Anubis (Egyptian), Hades (Greek)

There is MAGICK when you Play...

Get motivated to be healthy and fit
Get your body moving... and don't quit!
Get up and go out to play
No need to be cooped up indoors all day!

You could pretend to be a pirate on a ship that's sailing away,
Or travel over the frozen tundra on a dog sleigh.
You could pretend to be an astronaut and everyday
You seek out and explore new planets beyond the Milky Way.

Perhaps a game with an opposing team,
like bad mitten or baseball...
Maybe you prefer to put your energy
into swimming, soccer, or softball.

No matter what you choose to do...
Try different things till you find what is right for you!

YIN-YANG...

In the natural world, Yin-Yang or "Yin and Yang" represents the balance of opposing forces. Interacting as a greater whole, creating peace, harmony, and balance. They each have their own features and yet, within each one, there is a little piece of the other. Yin is the female aspect: nighttime, water, earth, moon, slow, cold, and wet. Yang is the male aspect: daytime, fire, sky, sun, fast, hot, and dry.

QUESTION: Why do you think Yin and Yang, each contain a small piece of the other?

Answers may vary: Because it creates balance within themselves

There is MAGICK in Hearing...

When we sit quietly listening... overhearing!

Listen to the wee Chickadee,
"Som'thin to eat... som'thin to eat" he calls out from his tree.

Hear the cranky Crow
Cry out to his mom, *"I know... I KNOW!"*

While the Grackel with his cackel,
Calls to the house cat, *"Kitty, Kitty... Kitty, Kitty"*

Listen to the leaves excitedly rustle about,
As they Congratulate the Oak on her newest little sprout.

And hear in the Wind, a gentle whispering...
"Believe in yourself... You can do anything!"

LEARNING TO LISTEN...

Sometimes it's just tree-top gossip that the birds are all a flutter about, but other times they give out warnings to anyone or anything that will listen. Animals, plants... everything has a language of its own, and when we stop and silence ourselves (inside and out)... when we listen with an open mind and a quiet soul... their sounds become translated into words that we know.

QUESTION: What is the name, for the practice, that we use to quiet ourselves, so that we can listen more clearly?

Answer: Meditation

There is MAGICK in an Apple...

Behold the hidden wonder
Seen only through minds without blunder,
Inside the system of seeds we are given a star...
Now, you won't see that in any fruit bar!

Go ahead... take a bite...
Enjoy the wonder with delight
Providing nourishment, without clout,
In this world and throughout

Delicious and nutritious!
Especially when eaten as a pie.
They're good for your body, so comply,
Pick them straight from a tree..
And eat them... one or two... or three!

AN APPLE A DAY... KEEPS THE SHAMAN AWAY!

Apples are a simple, spiritual, super fruit. They have a natural sugar for energy and provide vitamins and minerals like; A (an Antioxidant), B (for Brain function)... Plus, just as there are many different tastes in the world, there are as many deliciously different types of apples in a variety of colors like; McIntosh (red), Golden Delicious (yellow) and Granny Smith (green).

QUESTION: What other fruit is a super-healthy fruit and has been around since the beginning of time? (Hint: Its seeds were given to the Greek Goddess, Persephone)

Answer: Pomegranate

There is MAGICK in Books...

Open your mind and take a look.
Take a journey into a book.
Explore new worlds, new places
Plus some old and unusual spaces.

Set aside time... plan your destination...
Then go on an amazing adventurous dictation.

Find yourself a cozy little nook....
Become one with your book,
Breathe it in... see it, feel it... live it...
Take it to the end... don't give in, don't quit.
Be brave and courageous... be funny and smart....
For a good book will always live in your heart.

NEVER JUDGE A BOOK BY ITS COVER!

Be it a book, a person or an animal... you should never judge it by its cover, or on its appearance alone... because in the end, it's what's on the inside that counts. You never really know the whole story until you've read the whole story – staying with it until the end.

CHALLENGE: **If you were a book, what would your title be, what would the cover look like... how does it best represent you?**

There is MAGICK in Nature...

With all of its birds and bees... flowers and trees!

Along a dirt path, where the wildlife watches you from afar
And the birds chatter from dawn till night's first star...

Where the water babbles on... and on... from a busy brook
And rocks sparkle with treasure, tempting you to take a look...

The countless flowers in their brilliant colors can be seen,
Giving off a fragrance, infused with a thick evergreen...

The moss carpeting is like walking on sponge cake
Marking out the perfect place to take a quick break.

RECORD THE MOMENT!

You really shouldn't disturb nature (environments of plants) or mess with habitats (the homes of animals). But you can take pictures, paint, draw, write a poem or a little song to help keep your memory of that moment awake and alive. Sometimes you can take small samples of nature to keep – but only when an adult says its okay. You wouldn't want to get a poisonous itch!

QUESTION: There are 2 types of animals – DIURNAL animals that come out during the day and this other type of animal that comes out at night?

Answer: Nocturnal animals

There is MAGICK in a Hug...
When we first embrace... at the door...
on the welcoming rug.

There is MAGICK when we Hold the Hand...
Of a friend who feels overwhelmed...
with too much to withstand.

There is MAGICK when we Quietly Listen...
With our ears and an open mind,
while sipping juice of Alhuren.

There is MAGICK when we Talk Things Out...
Chattering in conversation...
getting all our feeling laid out.

There is MAGICK when all is Said and Done...
When we know without a doubt,
who our friends are... each and every one.

THE MOST AMAZING MEDICINE...

When used properly, herbs have the amazing ability to heal. From calming a cold to soothing your itches, there are herbs for just about everything. Though sometimes, the best medicine for what bothers you (or someone else) will not come from an herb, but from friends and family who can provide; an armful of love, a handful of time, a cup full of compassion and splash of humor... to get things feeling right.

QUESTION: Do you know what Alhuren is used for? (Hint: it's also known as Elder / Elder berries)

Answers may vary: To bless a person, place or thing... plus protection and healing

There is MAGICK in
Crystals, Stones & Gems...

If, in your pocket you keep... Ruby,
Then... confidence is offered to you, as a newbie.

If, in your pocket you keep... Tiger's eye,
Then... you will keep good luck nearby.

If, in your pocket you keep... Jet,
Then... you'll be protected from a threat.

If, in your pocket you keep... Coral,
Then... you're less likely to get into a quarrel.

If, in your pocket you keep... Aquamarine,
Then... you'll feel more relaxed and a bit serene.

LIVING ROCKS?!

Many people mistake rocks for being nothing more than rocks! But the truth is... they are a living object, in a manner of speaking – they give off energy, they have an aura similar to our own. That's why different crystals, gems, and stones have different properties, and what stone works for one person, may not work the same way for another person.

QUESTION: What are some of the crystals, stones, and gems used in healing and in meditations?

Answers may vary: Amber, Quartz, Hematite

There is MAGICK in Meditation...

When you are angry or confused,
When you are feeling frustrated or abused
And the sky is falling through...
Coming down in pieces all around you.

Sit quietly and close your eyes
Do it now... don't wait for a sunrise!

Find a place in your mind
Where you won't feel confined,
Put your breathing into cruise control,
And begin to heal your body, mind, and soul.

OM / AUM

During mediations some people chant Om, which is a sacred sound to the Hindus. It represents both aspects of God, symbolizing the infinite energy of the divine. It has 3 sounds A-U-M which is pronounced:"ah" which comes from the throat,"oo" rolls over the tongue, and "mm" comes across the lips... but you don't hold the sound, the word forever, you must let the sacred sound vibration go...

QUESTION: When is the best time to meditate and where is the best place to meditate?

Answers may vary: Anytime and Anyplace

There is MAGICK in Love and in Light...

Make a tight fist... keep it closed... feel the strain...
Remember that a closed heart will always have pain,
It brings you into a dark... dark place...
Keeping you from that... which you never want to face.

Now, Open your hand... feel it as it does revive...
Remember that an open heart is a soul that's alive...
Let it breathe... set it free from the tension... and the pain...
Because locking yourself up.... can cause such a strain.
Instead when life makes you feel horribly sad... or mad...
And you see it and feel it... in every which way that is bad...
Take a deep breath... let your troubles be cast aside...
Let your mind be at peace and open your arms wide...
Let the warmth of a heavenly hug... fill you with love and of light
Giving you peace of mind, that everything will be alright.

WARNING: DON'T FEED THE MONSTER!!!

Did you know it requires more energy, more time... to invite Hate in and make it into so much more. Hate needs to feed off you... so you have to keep supplying it with negative thinking and mean words. It convinces you that you can't live without it... that everything will fall apart... and things will get worse if you don't feed it... keeping it alive within you.... But Hate is sadly mistaken... no one needs Hate... or darkness in their heart!

CHALLENGE: To create Love... not Hate! To plant the seeds of Love and watch them grow... without the strain of Hate around to plant, to sow.

60

There is MAGICK in Butterflies...

See the little caterpillar... creeping along...
Oh so slow... all day long
Taking in his little world... learning all he can...
Hoping to be so much more... well, that's his plan!

Then one day, he realizes... that it's time,
He's ready to move on...
To find a place that's sublime...
That's were his chrysalis, he will form...
And through the long winter...
He will be safe and warm.

From within he will begin to make changes, growing inside...
Until at last, he emerges... having made a great stride...
And as he opens his wings... there is an awe-inspiring *sigh*...
Change is amazing... as he flutters away... high into the sky!

LEARN ... LIVE ... SHARE

Life is a process of transformation, of changing... of growing with lessons of learning, of knowledge. Like the caterpillar to chrysalis to butterfly... we as small children learn all that we can, then as young adults we begin to live our lives, finally as grandparents, we share our knowledge with our children's children, watching them to grow wings and soar high into the sky on their own.

QUESTION: Just because you are a caterpillar doesn't guarantee that you will become a Butterfly... what does the Wooly Bear Caterpillar change into?

Answer: the Isabella Tiger Moth

Glossary

Belief / Believe

To trust that things are true

Craft / The Craft

The practice of using personal energy with natural tools, to create change, without the religious standard (also known as: Folk Magick and/or Witchcraft)

Culture

A society or social group, at a particular time and place

Deity

God and Goddess

Dharma

Your reason for being, your purpose in life

Divination

The art of interpreting energy, signs, and/or symbols in order to give a reading.

Divine

Taking on properties of being a Deity, either in supernatural form or as an aspect

Endeavour

An undertaking that requires purpose, effort, and boldness

Esbat

The term used to include the four major Moon phase celebrations (Full Moon, Waxing, New Moon, Waning)

Ethics

A standard of conduct, morals, and values

Faith

Unquestionable belief in one or many Deities

Hearth

The center of ones home, the fireplace (or stove/kitchen)

Karma

How you live your life, with the knowledge that what you do in your lifetime (includes any previous lives too) is "boomeranged" back to you in the form of Quantum Energy

Magic

Slight of hand, parlor tricks

Magick

The movement of energy, for the purpose of creating change

Meditation

To calm yourself and have a chance to think clearly

Pagan

One who practices a Down to Earth/Earth-based way of living. (Also see Witch and Wiccan)

Quantum Energy

In reference to Spirituality it is also known as: Universal Energy, the Divine Power, or Spiritual Energy

Quest

The act of searching to accomplish a goal, an endeavour

Religion

A system of belief and worship with a code of ethics

Ritual

The behavior of a repeating custom exercises (like those of customary holiday observances and religious ceremonies)

Sabbot

The term used to include all of the eight Sun / Agricultural celebrations or traditions (Yule, Imbolc, Ostara, Beltane, Litha, Lughnasdh, Mabon, Samhain)

Sacred

Something that is considered special to or for the Gods.

Shaman

One who has a deeper consciousness or moral sense of the physical and spiritual world (also see Shamanism)

Shamanism

The practice of a Shaman using magick, rituals, and sometimes religion, to create change (also known as Shaman Healers and/or healers)

Soul

The spiritual, moral and emotional qualities of a person. Without form or body, the spirit of a person

Spirit

The human principle that includes thought, will, and life

Spiritual / Spirituality

Being of spirit, being sacred

Supernatural

Unexplainable forms, above and beyond the forces and laws of nature

Superstition

Something that is believed in, even if there is no rational thought, reasoning, or proven facts to back it up.

Trust

To depend on something or someone

Witch

One who practises in the way of the old crafts of home and of hearth (also see Pagan and Wiccan)

Wiccan

One who practices the ancient ways as a religion (also see Pagan and Witch)

Recommendations

Here are a few favorite books!

CHILDREN'S BOOKS

All I See Is Part of Me	Chara M. Curtis
Aidan's First Full Moon Circle	W. Lyon Martin
An Ordinary Girl – A Magical Child	W. Lyon Martin
The Elsie & Pooka Collection	Lora Gaddis
The Last Wild Witch	Starhawk
On My Way to a Happy Life	Deepak Chopra
Rabbit's Song	S. J. Tucker and Trudy Herring
Wild Child	Lynn Plourde

WORKBOOKS / FAMILY BOOKS

Circle Round	Starhawk, Diane Baker, Anne Hill
A Witch's Primer	Lorin Manderly
Pagan Degrees for Children	Shaddaramon
Growing Up Pagan	Raine Hill
Pagan Children's Workbook	Lady Eliana
My First Little Workbook of Wicca	Rev. V. Rieth

BOOKS FOR PARENTS

201 Little Buddhist Reminders	B. A. Kipfer
Animal Speak	Ted Andrews
Family Wicca	Ashleen O' Gaea
Magickal Crafts	Kristin Madden & Liz Roberts
Raising Witches	Ashleen O'Gaea
The Winter Solstice	John Matthews